Author:
John Malam studied ancient history and archaeology at the University of Birmingham, England, after which he worked as an archaeologist at the Ironbridge Gorge Museum in Shropshire. He is now an author, specialising in information books for children. He lives in Cheshire with his wife and their two children. Find out more at: www.johnmalam.co.uk

Artist:
David Antram was born in Brighton, England, in 1958. He studied at Eastbourne College of Art and then worked in advertising for fifteen years before becoming a full-time artist. He has illustrated many children's non-fiction books.

Series creator:
David Salariya was born in Dundee, Scotland. He has illustrated a wide range of books and has created and designed many new series for publishers in the UK and overseas. David established The Salariya Book Company in 1989. He lives in Brighton with his wife, illustrator Shirley Willis, and their son Jonathan.

Editor: **Stephen Haynes**

Editorial Assistant: **Mark Williams**

Published in Great Britain in 2008 by
Book House, an imprint of
The Salariya Book Company Ltd
25 Marlborough Place, Brighton BN1 1UB
www.salariya.com
www.book-house.co.uk

HB ISBN-13: 978-1-906370-19-0
PB ISBN-13: 978-1-906370-20-6

SALARIYA

1 3 5 7 9 8 6 4 2

A CIP catalogue record for this book is available from the British Library.

PAPER FROM
SUSTAINABLE
FORESTS

Printed and bound in China.
Printed on paper from sustainable sources.

Visit our website at **www.salariya.com**
for **free** electronic versions of:
You Wouldn't Want to be an Egyptian Mummy!
You Wouldn't Want to be a Roman Gladiator!
Avoid Joining Shackleton's Polar Expedition!
Avoid Sailing on a 19th-Century Whaling Ship!

Avoid working on the Statue of Liberty!

Written by
John Malam

Illustrated by
David Antram

Created and designed by
David Salariya

The Danger Zone

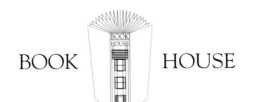

BOOK HOUSE

Contents

Introduction

The year is 1871, and you are in Paris, the capital of France. You work as a humble assistant to Frédéric Auguste Bartholdi, a sculptor who's becoming quite well known. He's been invited to meet Edouard de Laboulaye, a politician who loves the United States of America. It won't be the first time that Bartholdi has met him.

Six years ago, in 1865, Laboulaye told Bartholdi that he wanted to give a present to the USA from the people of France. Laboulaye thought it would be a good idea to give a statue to America. He said it would be a symbol of friendship between the two countries – but for years nothing came of the idea.

But things are different now, and Bartholdi thinks the statue might really go ahead. If it does, Bartholdi wants to be the sculptor to make it – and that will mean a lot of hard, sometimes dangerous work for you. *Bonne chance!* (Good luck!)

Vivent nos républiques! (Long live our republics!)

A statue? A big idea is born

How big? The man must be mad!

Edouard de Laboulaye has invited several important men to his house. He tells them about his idea of giving a statue to the people of America, and says it has to be ready in five years' time, by 1876. Why then? Because that's when the United States will be celebrating its 100th birthday. It became an independent country in 1776, and the statue will be a special birthday present. Laboulaye points to the figure of Liberty on the great seal of France. He wants to give the Americans their own Liberty statue – a monument to freedom. He has even thought of a name for it – rather a long one. As for the design of the statue, Bartholdi shocks everyone when he says he wants to build a colossus – a giant statue. You're really going to have your work cut out!

Inspiration

ALL TALK? Laboulaye first mentioned the idea to Bartholdi in 1865 – the year when the American Civil War ended. But so far it has been nothing more than an idea.

LIBERTAS AND LIBERTY. Bartholdi didn't just make up the design out of his own head. Other artists before him had imagined what Liberty might look like (see opposite).

1. ROMAN COINS. Libertas (Liberty), the goddess of freedom, was on them.

2. GREAT SEAL. Liberty is shown on the seal of the French Republic.

3. PAINTING. *The Republic Enlightening the World* (1848) by French artist A.-L. Janet-Lange.

Bon voyage! Off to America

Light out

EGYPT. In 1867 Bartholdi designed a giant lighthouse for Suez, Egypt. It was never built, but his design gave him ideas for the Statue of Liberty.

aboulaye needs to know what Americans think, so he sends Bartholdi on a fact-finding visit. You and another assistant go with him. You set off on 8 June 1871, and thirteen uncomfortable days later your ship sails into New York harbour. It passes Bedloe's Island, and Bartholdi thinks this would be a good place to put the statue. You spend the next three months trekking around the United States trying to drum up support, but Americans just aren't interested in the project. You really wish you'd stayed at home!

> I enjoyed your 'Hiawatha'.

Bartholdi on tour

THE BIG CITY. Bartholdi explores New York City, which he's heard so much about.

THE PRESIDENT. He meets Ulysses S. Grant, President of the United Sates of America.

THE POET. He also meets Henry Wadsworth Longfellow, America's most famous living poet.

Handy hint

Find your 'sea legs' as soon as you can. You'll be at sea for about two weeks, so you'll have to get used to it!

THE HARBOUR. If the statue goes on Bedloe's Island in New York harbour, everyone who arrives by sea will see it.

THE NATION. Bartholdi visits all these American cities to discuss his plans.

9

A giantess! Designing Liberty

My arm is aching.

Phrygian cap

Back in Paris, Bartholdi makes sketches and models of how Liberty might look. It's your job to help him work out his ideas, and sometimes you feel a bit silly...

He plans to make the statue about 45 metres (148 feet) high. It's meant to represent freedom, so he adds some freedom symbols. He tries a Phrygian cap – a hat worn in Roman times by ex-slaves who had gained their freedom. But not everyone would understand that, so he changes it to a crown with rays. He likes the idea of Liberty holding a broken chain – everyone knows that is a sign of freedom. But he changes that, too. It's so hard working with artists – they're never satisfied!

ROUGH IDEAS. These are some of the ideas that Bartholdi tries out before he settles on the final design.

Handy hint

Freeze! Do not forget your pose. Monsieur Bartholdi will ask you to stand in this exact position again and again and again!

Can't you keep your arm still?

Model mother?

MADAME BARTHOLDI. Some say that Bartholdi's mother, Charlotte, was the model for Liberty's face.

That's my boy!

Down the mine! A visit to Norway

Copper saint

GIANT STATUE. There is already a giant hollow statue made from copper. It's in Italy, and shows Saint Charles Borromeo. It was made in 1697.

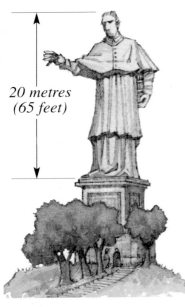

20 metres (65 feet)

The statue is far too big to be made from stone or solid metal. Bartholdi has decided to make it from thin sheets of copper, fixed to an iron frame. Even though it will be hollow, Liberty will still need 100 tonnes of pure copper, and there is only one place to get that from – the copper mines at Vigsnes in Norway. It's your job to go there and make sure that only the best copper is sent to Paris. You have to go down the mine and see the lumps of copper ore dug out of the rock. Then you watch as the ore is crushed and heated to produce liquid copper. It's hot, dangerous work – the copper fumes contain arsenic and other deadly poisons.

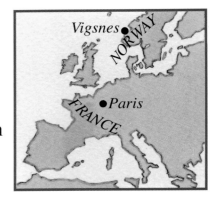

PURE COPPER. A rich vein of copper was discovered at Vigsnes in 1865, and the mine is now (in the 1870s) the leading producer in Europe.

Why copper?

SOFT. Copper can be beaten into shape more easily than other metals.

WILL NOT CRACK. Copper can be bent into shape without cracking.

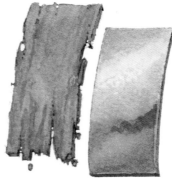

WILL NOT RUST. Iron rusts (left), but copper doesn't (right).

SELF-PROTECTING. Copper develops a protective greenish patina.

Who pays?

The money for the statue comes from:

A FRANCO-AMERICAN UNION set up by Laboulaye.

PEOPLE OF FRANCE. Towns collect people's money and send it off.

FRENCH BUSINESS PEOPLE. One man has sent 64 tonnes of copper.

SOUVENIRS. 200 mini statues are sold at 1,000 Francs ($350) each.

Plastered! Liberty takes shape

You thought the copper mines in Norway were bad enough, but now you're choking in plaster dust! At the workshop of Gaget, Gauthier & Co. in Paris, the air is full of it. Here a full-size model of Liberty is taking shape, bit by bit. Each piece starts off as a small clay model, then it's over to you to measure it. By doubling the measurements you make a model twice the size, and so on until you've reached Liberty's real size. You've got to take thousands of measurements, and you can't afford to get any of them wrong. The full-size pieces, made of wood, then have to be covered in plaster.

PIECE BY PIECE. Bartholdi divides the statue into about 310 sections; it takes 38 pieces to make the right hand and torch. Measurements have to be taken at many different points. Each section needs about 9,000 measurements, which can then be scaled up to make full-size models. This scaling-up technique is called 'pointing up'.

Starting small

1. SCALE MODEL. The maquette (as sculptors call it) is made from clay. It's one-sixteenth the size of the actual statue.

2. SECTION. A larger model is made of each part – one-quarter the size of the actual statue.

3. ACTUAL SIZE. Each section is scaled up to the size it will really be.

1

Strings called plumb lines are used as a guide for measuring. A metal weight makes the string hang exactly vertical.

Plumb line

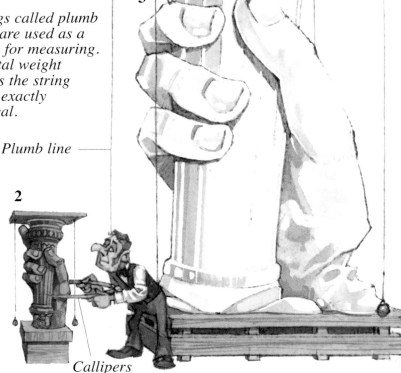

3

2

Callipers

Moulded! Liberty in wood

As if the plastering wasn't hard enough, the next job is really tricky. Now you've got to shape huge wooden moulds that fit exactly onto the outside of each plaster section. The shapes are complicated, and it takes skill to make the moulds fit around them. You mustn't leave any gaps between the wood and the plaster, or the copper sheets won't fit together once they've been beaten into shape. Remember the carpenter's golden rule: measure twice, cut once.

Careful! No gaps, please.

TOOLS OF THE TRADE.
A carpenter's chest contains his woodworking tools. You'll find planes for smoothing, braces and bits for boring holes, chisels for cutting, and a square for marking out right-angles.

I'm doing my best, sir!

Handy hint

Watch the chisel, not the mallet! If you take your eyes off it for a second, you'll be sorry...

!*%$*!!

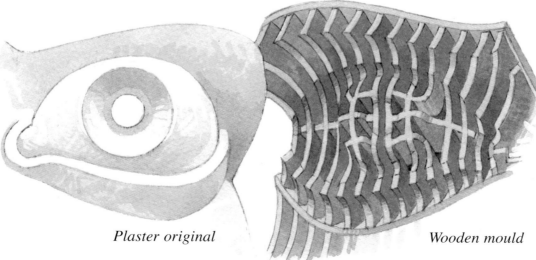

Plaster original

Wooden mould

TIGHT FIT. Here's part of the mould for one of Liberty's eyes. It's called a 'negative impression' – an inside-out version of the plaster original.

Hammered! Liberty's copper skin

The wooden moulds are taken into the fabrication room, which is where Liberty's copper skin is knocked into shape. Spend too long in here, and you could easily go deaf. Flat sheets of copper are laid onto each mould. They're placed on the side of the mould that was shaped to fit around the plaster section. The sheets are then beaten with hammers until they are pressed and bent into the shape of the mould. The beaten copper sheets are now the exact shapes needed for the statue – you hope!

For complicated shapes, the copper must be heated in a forge until it is soft – which means more of those dangerous fumes.

Right-hand men

HOLES. Endless rows of holes have to be drilled along the edges of the finished sheets of copper. These holes are for the rivets that will join the sheets together. More rivets will fix the copper sheets to the armature (right).

When you're drilling metal, watch out for the sharp metal shavings that come out of the hole. If a piece gets in your eye, you could be blinded.

Been.

Been who?

Knock Knock!

Been knocking so long, my head hurts!

Handy hint

The copper sheets that have been in the forge will be too hot to handle! Wear gloves so you don't burn your fingers.

Armature

Rivet

BIG HAND. Here's the right hand after all the moulded copper pieces have been joined together like a three-dimensional jigsaw puzzle. The torch is 6.4 metres (21 feet) long.

ARMATURE. The statue's armature or 'skeleton' is a network of iron bars fitted to the backs of the copper sheets. The sheets are fixed to the bars with rivets or bolts.

19

Torch bearer! Hand across the sea

Hand on tour

1876: PHILADELPHIA. Liberty's right hand and torch are displayed at the Philadelphia Centennial Exhibition. Thousands of people pay to climb inside.

1877: NEW YORK. After Philadelphia the hand travels to New York, where it goes on show in Madison Square. It stays there for four years.

t's now 1876, but Liberty isn't ready for America's 100th birthday celebrations! All that's finished is the right hand. It'll have to do, so it's shipped over from France to the US. It goes on show in Philadelphia, before moving to New York. It's your second visit to America, and you and Bartholdi have got much to do. Last time you came here, no-one was interested – but you're hoping the giant hand will change their minds. You've got to convince them to raise money for the massive pedestal that Liberty will stand on. If you can't do that, the whole project could fail.

Meanwhile, back in Paris...

1878: HEAD AND SHOULDERS. Liberty's head and shoulders are completed. They're put on show at the Universal Exposition in Paris. Inside is a winding staircase, and visitors pay to climb up to the windows in the crown.

1880: IRON SKELETON. French engineer Gustave Eiffel (he'll be famous one day for his tower) designs the iron framework or armature on which Liberty's copper skin will hang.

It wasn't this colour in Paris.

Copper soon tarnishes. One day Liberty will be green!

1882: HANDED BACK. After being in America for six years, Liberty's right hand is shipped back to France so it can be joined to the rest of the statue.

1884: ABOVE THE ROOFTOPS. Liberty is finished! The statue is fully assembled and towers over the roofs of Paris. Crowds of Parisians come to look.

On a pedestal! Liberty's island home

STAR FORT. Fort Wood is an old army fort on Bedloe's Island. Built in 1811, it is in the shape of a star with eleven points. Liberty's pedestal will go here.

HOSPITAL. In 1861, during the American Civil War, Fort Wood was used as a hospital for sick and wounded Confederate prisoners. Also, travellers who arrived in America with contagious diseases were kept on the island until they were better.

n 1877 the government of the United States agrees that Liberty can be put up on Bedloe's Island. The giant statue will stand in the centre of an old fort, on a concrete and stone pedestal built by American architect Richard Morris Hunt. This is the good news. The bad news is that the project to build the pedestal keeps running out of money, and when that happens building work stops. You've just got to stay calm and hope that enough money will be raised to finish building the base. If that doesn't happen, all your hard work will have been for nothing.

1884: Laying the cornerstone

AND FINALLY: Wheat, wine and oil are sprinkled over the stone. They symbolise plenty, gladness and peace.

SILVER TROWEL. The mortar is spread with a ceremonial trowel.

TIME CAPSULE. Coins, medals and newspapers are buried under the stone.

SQUARE AND TRUE. After the stone has been positioned it's checked to make sure it's perfectly level.

The base will soon be ready.

It had better be!

The pedestal, with its foundation, is almost exactly the same height as the statue itself. From the foundation to the tip of the flame will be 93 metres (305 feet).

Possible pedestals

ROUGH IDEAS. Bartholdi came up with several ideas for the pedestal. He thought Liberty could stand on a pyramid-shaped base, or on top of a tall tower. Neither idea went ahead.

Pyramid

Tower

Shipped! Liberty to America

In December 1884 the time comes for Liberty to begin her voyage to America. In Paris, the giant statue is taken apart and the pieces are packed into 214 crates, all clearly numbered. A train takes them to the port of Rouen, where it takes seventeen days for the heavy boxes to be stowed on board ship. It's not all plain sailing! The crossing is a slow and stormy one. In New York, some of the crates are damaged when they're unloaded. But worst of all, the pedestal's still not ready! The crates have to go into storage – and that costs money.

Sixty-five...

Are they having me on?

Coast to coast

ATLANTIC CROSSING. The crates are loaded onto the French steamship *Isère*. It sails from Rouen on 21 May 1885 and reaches New York 28 days later on 17 June.

STORMY WEATHER. The first part of the crossing is stormy and the ship uses up most of its coal. It has to stop at the Azores islands to load up with more.

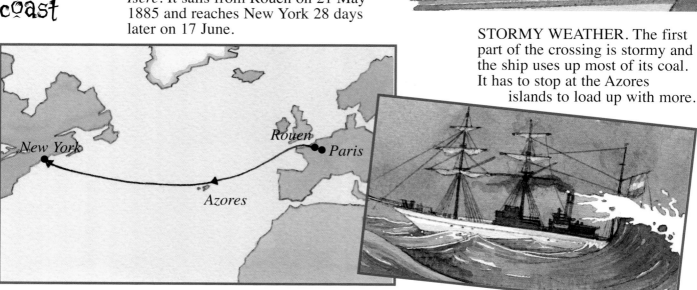

New York

Rouen

Paris

Azores

STACK 'EM HIGH. The crates are stacked on Bedloe's Island, where they will remain almost a year until the pedestal is ready.

PEDESTAL FINISHED. The campaign to raise funds for the pedestal is helped by newspaper owner Joseph Pulitzer. Readers of his paper give $102,000. On 22 April 1886, as the last block of stone is put in place for the pedestal, workers throw silver coins into the mortar. At last it is time for Liberty to take her place.

Standing tall! Liberty rising

Putting it all together

UNPACKED. Liberty's copper sheets are taken from their packing crates. Each piece is labelled so the Americans know where to fit them.

REPAIRS. Some pieces are found to be damaged and have to be repaired.

Soon after the pedestal is finished, Liberty's iron skeleton begins to take shape above it. By August 1886 it is ready for the statue's copper skin to be fixed. As the sheets are riveted in place, Liberty's giant body grows from the feet up. Finally, on a rainy day in October 1886, a big idea that had started twenty-one years earlier in France is finished in America. There are parades and speeches, fireworks and gunfire, and Frédéric Auguste Bartholdi unfurls the flag of France from the crown of the Statue of Liberty.

Will it fit?

RIVETS. The copper sheets have to be riveted to Eiffel's armature by hand – a noisy, back-breaking job. The first two rivets are named 'Bartholdi' and 'Pulitzer'!

ON THE INSIDE. Riveters have to climb up the iron armature inside the statue. When the sun shines on the copper, it gets unbearably hot inside.

ON THE OUTSIDE. There is no scaffolding – workers have to dangle on ropes up to 93 metres (305 feet) above the ground. Amazingly, there are no serious accidents.

Pardon?

Handy hint

Keep checking the drawings to make sure you know where all the 300-plus pieces of copper fit.

THE BIG DAY. On 28 October 1886, Bartholdi drapes a French flag from Liberty's crown. At last the giant statue is finished!

I don't like heights, but I'm putting a brave face on it.

It's about time!

Colossus! Liberty fact file

It didn't take long for the Statue of Liberty to become world-famous. Staring out to sea in the direction of Europe, she soon became a symbol of the United States. For tens of thousands of people who left Europe to begin new lives across the Atlantic, the light from Liberty's torch was a welcoming sight as their ships sailed into New York harbour.

AT THE TOP. Twelve people at a time could stand in the torch gallery (now closed).

ALL THE SEVENS. The crown, or nimbus, has seven rays – one for each continent.

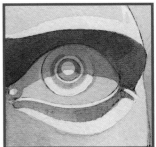

STAIRCASE. The spiral staircase inside the statue and pedestal has 354 steps.

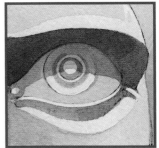

EYES WIDE OPEN. Each eye is 76cm (2ft 6in) wide.

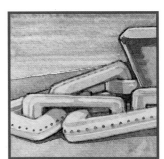

CHAINS. Broken chains representing freedom lie at Liberty's right foot.

WORLD'S TALLEST. In 1886 the Statue of Liberty was said to be the world's tallest monument.

Note: only the tops of the monuments are shown here.

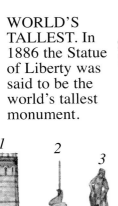

1 Victory Monument, New Delhi, India
2 Tower of San Martino, near Sirmione, Italy
3 Hercules Monument, Kassel, Germany
4 Bennington Battle Monument, Vermont, USA
5 Victory Monument, Berlin, Germany
6 War Monument, Indiana, USA

7 Emperor Wilhelm Monument, Kyffhäuser Mountain, Germany
8 Garfield Memorial, Ohio, USA
9 Scheldt Freedom Monument, Antwerp, Belgium
10 Wellington Obelisk, Dublin, Ireland

LONG NOSE. Liberty's nose measures 110cm (3ft 8in) long.

TABLET. The date is 4 July 1776 – the date of the Declaration of Independence.

WAY IN. There's a doorway in the sole of the right foot.

POEM. Emma Lazarus's poem about the statue, 'The New Colossus', is engraved on a bronze plaque inside Liberty's pedestal. The most famous lines are: 'Give me your tired, your poor, / Your huddled masses yearning to breathe free,' – a reference to immigrants from Europe coming to live in the United States.

TORCH. On 1 November 1886, lights inside the torch were switched on and Liberty became a lighthouse. A new torch, which doesn't light up, was fitted in 1986. On a windy day the torch can sway as much as 13cm (5 inches).

NAME CHANGE. In 1956 Bedloe's Island was officially renamed Liberty Island.

It took about twenty years for Liberty's copper to turn green.

Glossary

Armature A framework or skeleton of metal or wood inside a statue. Its purpose is to support the statue.

Callipers A device like a pair of compasses with curved legs. It is used to measure the exact width of an object or an opening, especially when the shape is too complicated to measure with a ruler.

Colossus A giant or colossal statue, much larger than life-size.

Contagious disease A disease that can be spread by coming into close contact with an infected person.

Copper A reddish-yellow metal that is fairly soft and easy to work.

Declaration of Independence The document signed on 4 July 1776 which declared that the United States of America were no longer British colonies.

Forge A fire in which metal is heated until it's soft enough to reshape.

Maquette A scale model of a statue made by the artist. It's used as a guide to making the full-size statue.

Mould (noun) A shape from which further identical shapes can be made.

Mould (verb) To form something into a particular shape.

Nimbus In art, a halo around the head of a figure.

Ore A rock containing natural minerals from which metal can be extracted.

Patina A coating which forms naturally on metal as it ages, and helps to protect it from corrosion. The patina on copper is bluish-green, and is sometimes called **verdigris**.

Pedestal A base on which a statue stands; also called a **plinth**.

Plaster of Paris A white paste made from gypsum (a chalk-like substance), used for moulding and model-making.

Plumb line A string with a weight on the end to make it hang vertically. It's used as a guide when measuring.

Pointing up The process of taking measurements from a scale model in order to work out the size and shape of the actual statue.

Republic A type of government in which the country's leaders are chosen by the people.

Rivet A short metal rod used to fasten two or more pieces of metal together. The ends of the rivet are beaten with a hammer while the rivet is hot. This makes the ends swell outwards so the rivet cannot fall out of its hole.

Scaffolding A temporary framework put up around a structure while it is being built.

Seal A metal disc which is used to stamp a medal-like design in a piece of wax. The wax impression can be attached to an official document to show that it is real, and not a fake.

31

Index